Steck-Vaughn

English ASAP™

Connecting English to the Workplace

SCANS Consultant

Shirley Brod
Spring Institute for International Studies
Boulder, Colorado

Program Consultants

Judith Dean-Griffin
ESL Teacher
Windham Independent School District
Texas Department of Criminal Justice
Huntsville, Texas

Marilyn K. Spence
Workforce Education Coordinator
Orange Technical Education Centers
Mid-Florida Tech
Orlando, Florida

Brigitte Marshall
English Language Training
for Employment Participation
Albany, California

Dennis Terdy
Director, Community Education
Township High School District 214
Arlington Heights, Illinois

Christine Kay Williams
ESL Specialist
Towson University
Baltimore, Maryland

STECK-VAUGHN
C O M P A N Y

A Division of Harcourt Brace & Company

Acknowledgments

Executive Editor:	Ellen Northcutt
Supervising Editor:	Tim Collins
Assistant Art Director:	Richard Balsam
Interior Design:	Richard Balsam, Jill Klinger, Paul Durick
Electronic Production:	Jill Klinger, Stephanie Stewart, David Hanshaw, Alan Klemp
Assets Manager:	Margie Foster

Editorial Development: Course Crafters, Inc., Newburyport, Massachusetts

Photo Credits

Alhadeff-p.3, 9, 41, 43d, 49, 68a, 68b; Don Couch Photography-p.25, 33c, 33d; Jack Demuth-p.43b, 75; Patrick Dunn-p.43a; Christine Galida-p.1, 21c, 21d, 43c; Park Street-p.21a, 21b, 33a, 33b, 65, 68c; Daniel Thompson Photography-p.4.

Illustration Credits

Cover: Tim Dove, D Childress
Cindy Aarvig-p.10, 14b, 17, 58, 71a; Meg Aubrey-p.18a, 59; Richard Balsam-p.11, 12, 14a, 15, 26e, 57 (signs), 60, 62 (signs), 64; Barbara Beck-p.50; Antonio Castro-p.34; Chris Celusniak-p.42; David Griffin-p.35, 44b, 70b-e; Dennis Harms -p.20; Laura Jackson-p.18b-e; Chuck Joseph-p.4, 6, 7, 8, 16, 24, 26a-d, 27, 29, 31a, 38, 39d, 40, 44a, 46, 51, 52, 53, 54, 55; Linda Kelen-p.63, 67; Annie Matsick-p.57i, 57j, 61, 73; Gordon Ricke-p.2, 19, 22b, 23, 39a-c; John Scott-p.36; Charles Shaw-p.57a-h, 62g-j, 66, 74; kreativ-design/ Danielle Szabo-p.22a, 28, 30, 31b, 32, 70a, 71b, 71c, 76, 78, 79.

ISBN 0-8172-7956-3

Contents

To the Student and the Teacher

Every unit of this Workbook has one or more exercises for each section of the Student Book. Use this chart to find the exercise(s) for each section. For example, after the "Talk About It" page, do all the exercises with a 3, such as 3 or 3A, 3B, 3C, etc.

Student Book Section	All Workbook Exercises with the Number
Unit Opener	1
Getting Started	2
Talk About It	3
Keep Talking	4
Listening	5
Grammar	6
Reading and Writing	7
Extension	8
Performance Check	9

Communication

1A. CIRCLE

Circle *yes* or *no*.

1. Her name's Linda.   (yes)   no

2. His name's Dan.   yes   no

3. They're saying hello.   yes   no

4. They work in an office.   yes   no

5. They're construction workers. yes   no

1B. WRITE

Write the names of some of your coworkers, classmates, or friends.

_____   _____

_____   _____

Match the person to the job. Write the letter.

~~**a.**~~ waitress   **b.** truck driver   **c.** construction worker

1. My name's Manuel.   **2.** My name's Kara.   **3.** My name's Kee.

2B. WRITE

Complete the sentences. Use the information from 2A and the words below. Then write about yourself.

~~**Korean**~~   **Russian**   **Spanish**

1. Kee's from Korea. He speaks _____Korean_____.

He's a _____truck driver_____.

2. Kara's from Russia. She speaks _____.

She's a _____.

3. Manuel's from Mexico. He speaks _____.

He's a _____.

4. I'm from _____. I speak _____.

I'm a _____.

2C. WRITE

Complete the chart about the people in 2B.

Name	Country	Language	Job
1. Kee	Korea	Korean	truck driver
2.			
3.			
4.			

3. MATCH

What does Maria say next? Write the letter.

1. **Kara:** Hi, I'm Kara, the new waitress.

   Maria: _c_

2. **Kara:** It's nice to meet you, Maria.

   Maria: _____

3. **Kara:** Where are you from?

   Maria: _____

a. I'm from Mexico.

b. Nice to meet you, too.

~~c.~~ Hello. My name's Maria.

4. COMPLETE THE DIALOG

from	nice
~~Hi~~	nice
like	too
meet	

A _____ Hi _____, I'm John. I'm a mechanic.

B It's _____ to meet you, John. I'm Fidel.
I'm the new driver.

A Nice to _____ you, _____, Fidel.

I'd _____ you to meet Marta. She's one of our dispatchers.

C It's _____ to meet you, Fidel. Where are you from?

B I'm _____ El Salvador.

5. CIRCLE

Complete the dialog. Circle the letter.

1. Hi, my name's Jacob. What's your name?

   a. I'm a truck driver.

   (b.) My name's Leon.

2. It's nice to meet you, Leon.

   a. It's nice to meet you, too.

   b. Good morning.

3. Leon, I'd like you to meet Pablo.

   a. I speak Spanish.

   b. It's nice to meet you, Pablo.

6A. WRITE

Complete each sentence.

I	am	from Chicago.
He	is	
She		
It		
We	are	
You		
They		

Ana Velez
Truck Driver

Tom Wang
Mechanic

1. She ___is___ a truck driver.

2. Her name _____ Ana.

3. Tom _____ a mechanic.

4. They _____ employees at Action Trucking.

Unit 1

6B. WRITE

Complete each sentence.

I + am = I'm	We + are = We're
He + is = He's	You + are = You're
She + is = She's	They + are = They're

1. They **'re** bus drivers.

2. We _____ English students.

3. She _____ a mail clerk.

4. You _____ an employee at Action Trucking.

6C. WRITE

Complete the sentences about yourself.

1. Where are you from?

   I _____ from _____.

2. What job do you do?

   I _____ a/an _____.

6D. COMPLETE

I	my
he	his
she	her
it	its
we	our
you	your
they	their

My last name is Ramos.

1. Hi, **my** (**my, her**) name's Maria. I'm from Costa Rica.

2. I'd like you to meet our new cook. He's from Costa Rica, too.

   _____ (**His, Their**) name is Pablo.

3. We live on Green Street. _____ (**Their, Our**) neighborhood is very nice.

4. _____ (**Our, Their**) neighbors are from Russia. _____ (**His, Their**) son

   also works here.

Unit 1

Read the application. Circle *yes* or *no*.

Pizza Palace   **Application for Employment**

Name: __Long__ ___Carmen___   Date: _____
     Last   First

Address: __23__ __Western Avenue_____
     Number   Street

__Los Angeles__ __CA__ __98543__
   City   State   Zip Code

Telephone number: __555-7980_____
     Area Code   Number

Languages you speak: __English and Spanish_____

Job you are applying for: __cook_____

1. Carmen lives in Los Angeles.   (yes) no

2. She speaks Spanish.   yes no

3. Her zip code is 78523.   yes no

4. She wants to be a cook.   yes no

Carmen is not ready to turn in her application. Help her to complete the form. What two things does she need to add?

_____

_____

Make a list of information to put on this application.

1. _____date_____   2. _____

3. _____   4. _____

5. _____   6. _____

You are applying for a new job. Complete the job application.

Pizza Palace   **Application for Employment**

Name: _____ Date: _____
         Last   First

Address: _____
           Number   Street

_____
   City   State   Zip Code

Telephone number: _____
                   Area Code   Number

Languages you speak: _____

Job you are applying for: _____

DO NOT WRITE BELOW THIS LINE
....
Interviewer's comments

_____
_____
_____
_____
_____

7D. CHECK YOUR WORK

Look at the job application in 7C. Is it OK? Put a check (✔) for each thing that's OK.

_____ **1.** Everything is spelled correctly.

_____ **2.** The application is complete. All the items are filled.

_____ **3.** The handwriting is neat. You can read everything.

There is a part of the application you do not fill in. Who do you think fills it in?

_____

Unit 1

Fill in the form. Answer the questions.

F *Farrel Company*

Fill in the following information for your employee ID badge. Return the completed form to the Human Resources Department.

Name: _____

Job: _____

Signature: _____

Date: _____

1. What is the form for?

   _____

2. Where do you return the completed form?

   _____

Check the skills you learned in this unit.

❏ 1. Introduce yourself

❏ 2. Make introductions

❏ 3. Complete forms for work

Look at the skills you checked.
Which ones can help you at work? Write the numbers. _____

Your Workplace

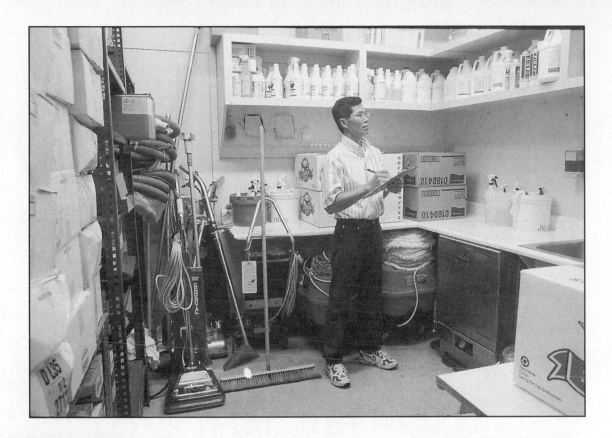

1A. CIRCLE

Look at the picture. Read the question. Circle the answer.

1. Where is the man?   the break room   (the supply room)   the parking lot

2. Is there a supply room at your workplace or school?   yes   no

3. What's usually in a supply room?   boxes   cars   exits

1B. WRITE

Write places at your workplace or school.

1._____   2._____

3._____   4._____

5._____   6._____

Where do you find these things? Write the place on the line.

~~break room~~ meeting room office parking lot rest room supply room

1. __break room__ 2. _____ 3. _____

4. _____ 5. _____ 6. _____

2B. COMPLETE THE CHART

Write about your workplace or school.

Place	Things in That Place
supply room	boxes

Unit 2

3A. CIRCLE

Where do you usually go? Circle the places. Add two places to the floor plan.

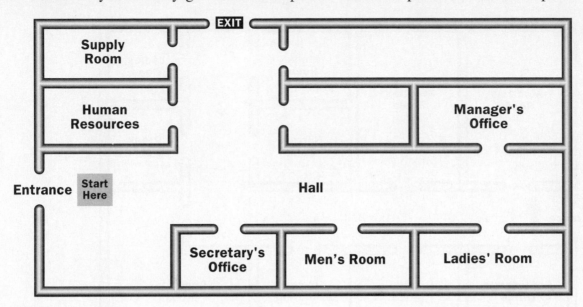

3B. WRITE

Complete the sentences. Use the floor plan in 3A.

first   left   ~~left~~   right   third   down

1. John needs to go to human resources.

   Turn _____left_____. Human resources is the _____

   door on the _____.

2. Lin needs to go to the ladies' room.

   Walk _____ the hall. The ladies' room is the _____

   door on the _____.

4. GIVE DIRECTIONS

Complete the dialog. Follow the example. Write about your workplace or school.

1. **A** Where's the _____ *supply room* _____?

   B It's _____ *down the hall on the right* _____.

2. **A** Where's the _____?

   B It's _____.

3. **A** Where's the _____?

   B It's _____.

Unit 2

5. WRITE

Look at the floor plan. Read the sentences. Write the room.

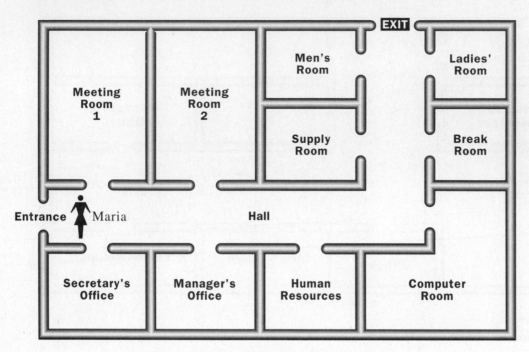

1. It's next to the secretary's office. _____ *the manager's office* _____

2. It's between the computer room and the ladies' room. _____

3. It's on the right next to the exit. _____

4. It's next to meeting room 1. _____

6A. ANSWER THE QUESTIONS

Use the floor plan in 5. Answer the questions.

Am	I	in the hall?
Is	he	
	she	
	it	
Are	we	
	you	
	they	

Yes,	I	am.
	he	is.
	she	
	it	
	we	are.
	you	
	they	

No,	I'm	not.
	he	isn't.
	she	
	it	
	we	aren't.
	you	
	they	

1. Is the men's room next to the supply room? _____ *Yes, it is.* _____

2. Are the rest rooms down the hall from the supply room? _____

3. Is the break room next to the entrance? _____

4. Is the exit down the hall from the supply room? _____

Unit 2

Write questions and answers about the floor plan on page 12.

Where's	the exit? the supply room?

The exit is	down the hall. across the hall from the rest rooms. next to the break room. between the break room and the ladies' room.

1. (men's room) ___ Where's the men's room? ___
   ___ It's next to the supply room. ___

2. (manager's office) _____

   _____

3. (break room) _____

   _____

4. (meeting room 1) _____

   _____

5. (computer room) _____

   _____

6C. WRITE DIRECTIONS

Tell Maria how to get to the break room. Use the floor plan on page 12.

Go	down the hall. to the supply room.

~~Go~~	Turn	Walk	Left	Right

___ Go down the hall. ___

_____

_____

Unit 2

Miguel's boss asked him to get these things from the supply room. They're for the guests in room 1610 of the hotel.

HOTEL CALIFORNIA

Room 1610

1 bottle of shampoo   1 pillow

6 towels   1 box of chocolates

1 trash can

4 glasses

Look at the picture. Miguel is taking these things to room 1610.

Check the list. What's not here? Write it on the line. _____

7B. WRITE

You're the manager of your department at work.
Write a to-do list for the employees.

Look at your list again. What do the employees do first? Second? Last?
Number the items. Start with 1.

7C. WRITE

Write your to-do list for work, school, or home.

My To-Do List

Unit 2

Where do the people go? Read the directory. Read the sentences.
Write the suite number.

3440 Port Street Building

	Suite
Discount City Superstores	
Executive Offices	300
Purchasing	330
Human Resources	320
Reliable Office Supplies	150
Dr. Li Park, M.D.	170
West Construction Company	
Sales	250
Operations	260
Human Resources	270

1. Clark wants a job at Discount City Superstores. Suite __320__

2. Ana needs some pens and pencils. Suite _____

3. Eric is delivering supplies to the sales office of West Construction

Company. Suite _____

4. Chen wants to see the manager of Discount City Superstores. Suite _____

5. Martin has an appointment with Dr. Park. Suite _____

9. THINK ABOUT YOUR LEARNING

Check the skills you learned in this unit.

❏ **1.** Give directions to places at work

❏ **2.** Understand directions to places at work

❏ **3.** Name places at work

❏ **4.** Use a to-do list

Look at the skills you checked.
Which ones can help you at work? Write the numbers. _____

Unit 2

Technology

1A. MATCH

Write the letter next to the name of the machine.

___c___ **1.** copier

_____ **2.** table saw

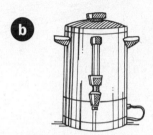

_____ **3.** cash register

_____ **4.** coffee maker

1B. WRITE

Write the names of three machines you use at work, school, or home.

_____

_____

_____

Write the number in the circle next to each machine.

1. printer   **2.** calculator   **3.** fax machine

4. telephone   **5.** computer   **6.** stapler

2B. WRITE

Write what you can do with each machine.   add   make   send   ~~write~~

1. ___write a letter___   2. _____

3. _____   4. _____

3. LABEL

Label the parts of the copier.

START button **cover** **glass**

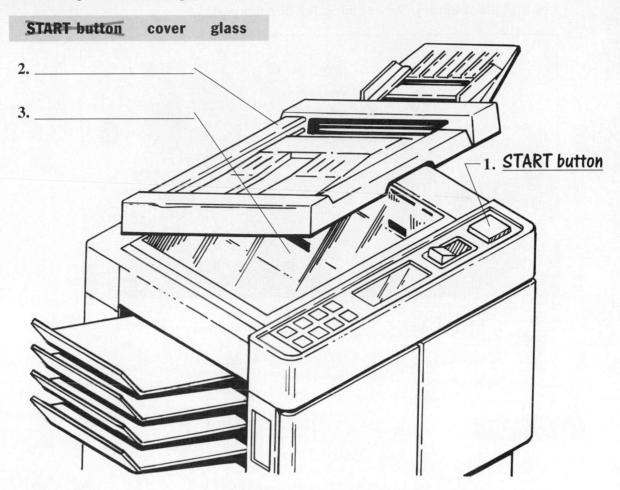

2. _____

3. _____

1. <u>START button</u>

4. WRITE

Write the steps for using a copier.

close **choose** **open** **press** **put**

Steps: 1. _____ *Open the cover.* _____

2. _____

3. _____

4. _____

5. _____

Unit 3

Your manager wants you to learn how to use the new cash register.
Look at the diagram. Write the letter of each part.

___d___ **1.** ENTER key   _____ **2.** keypad

_____ **3.** ON key   _____ **4.** drawer

6A. WRITE

Complete the sentences.

I'm	reading the instructions.		I'm not		reading the instructions.
He's			He	isn't	
She's			She		
We're			We	aren't	
You're			You		
They're			They		

1. He _'s telling_____ (**tell**) us how to use the new electric drills.

2. We _____ (**clean**) the break room now.

3. She _____ (**not go**) to work this morning. She has a doctor's appointment.

4. They _____ (**work**) at the warehouse today.

5. I _____ (**not start**) my machine. I think it's broken.

6. He _____ (**repair**) the copier.

7. She _____ (**talk**) to a customer on the telephone.

What are the people doing? Write questions and answers.

Am	I	pushing the right button?
Is	he	
	she	
Are	we	
	you	
	they	

Yes,	you	are.
No,		aren't.

What	are you	doing?
Where		going?

What is she doing?

She's fixing a car.

Write more questions and answers about the pictures.

1. **Is she fixing a car? Yes, she is.**

2. _____

3. _____

4. _____

Unit 3

6C. WRITE

Write the word. Use *'s* or *s'*.

1. The _____secretary's_____ (**secretary**) office is down the hall.

2. It's next to the _____ (**manager**) office.

3. The _____ (**job counselors**) office is next to the supply room.

7A. WRITE

Look at the diagram of a vacuum cleaner. Write the part you use for each step.

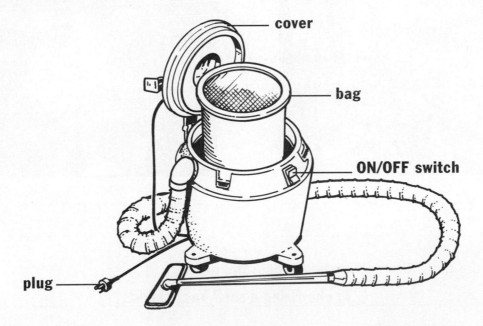

1. You open it to put in a new bag. _____the cover_____

2. You press it to turn on the vacuum cleaner. _____

3. You change it when it is full. _____

4. You press it to turn off the vacuum cleaner. _____

Unit 3

Look at the pictures of a coffee maker. Write the instructions.

Pour   ~~Plug in~~   Press   Put

1

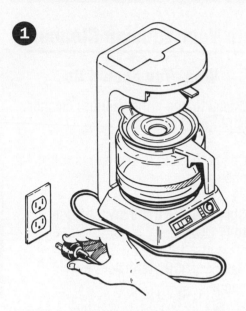

Plug in the coffee maker.
_____

2

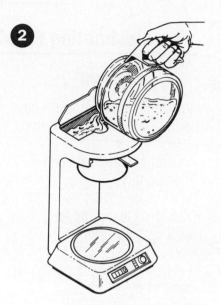

_____
_____

3

_____
_____

4

_____
_____

What do you do if there's a problem? Read the instructions.
Answer the questions.

Troubleshooting Problems with Your Vacuum Cleaner

Problem		What You Should Do
Vacuum cleaner doesn't start when I press the ON button.	→	Check to see if the vacuum cleaner is plugged in.
Vacuum cleaner doesn't pick up dirt.	→	Check the bag. If the bag is full, change it.
Vacuum cleaner doesn't work well on hard floors.	→	Check to see if the switch is set to FLOORS.
I cannot find vacuum cleaner bags at my store.	→	Call 555-9090 to order new bags.

1. How can you get new bags? _____ *You call 555-9090.* _____

2. What can you do if the vacuum cleaner isn't picking up dirt? _____

_____

3. What can you do if the vacuum cleaner isn't working well on hard floors?

_____

9. THINK ABOUT YOUR LEARNING

Check the skills you learned in this unit.

❏ 1. Listen to and follow instructions

❏ 2. Set up and use a machine

❏ 3. Read a diagram

❏ 4. Explain how to use a machine

Look at the skills you checked.
Which ones can help you at work? Write the numbers. _____

Time Management

1A. WRITE

Look at the picture. Write *yes* or *no*.

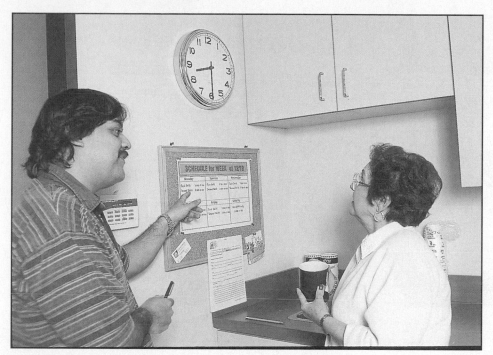

1. They are at work. **yes**

2. They are looking at a work schedule. _____

3. A work schedule tells the days people work. _____

4. A work schedule tells the times people work. _____

1B. WRITE THE ANSWERS

Write about your school or work schedule.

1. What days do you work or go to school?

_____

2. What time do you get to work or school?

_____

3. What time do you leave?

_____

2. WRITE

Look at the clocks. Write the times.

1

12:45

2

_____

3

_____

4

_____

3A. WRITE

Look at the calendar. Write the days.

March

Sunday	Monday	Tuesday	Wednesday	Thursday	Friday	Saturday
		1	2	3	4	5
6	7	8	9	10	11	12

1. March 1 = _____Tuesday_____ **2.** March 6 = _____

3. March 7 = _____ **4.** March 10 = _____

5. March 11 = _____ **6.** March 12 = _____

Unit 4

Look at Elena's calendar. Complete the sentences.

October

Sunday	Monday	Tuesday	Wednesday	Thursday	Friday	Saturday
12	13 **Lunch with Sylvia 12:30**	14 **English class 4:30**	15	16 **8:30 Conference with John's teacher**	17	18 **Day off**
19	20	21	22	23	24	25

1. Elena is having lunch with Sylvia on _____Monday_____.

2. She has a conference with John's teacher on _____.

3. She has English class on _____.

4. Elena wants to meet you for lunch. What day can you both meet?

_____.

Do you have any appointments this week? _____

Write the days and times of your appointments. _____

_____

Choose the word to complete each sentence. Write it on the line.

~~appointment~~   **At**   **late**   **Thanks**   **time**

A I'd like to leave early on Friday. I have a doctor's _____appointment_____.

B What _____ do you want to leave?

A _____ 2:00.

B That's fine. Can you stay _____ on Thursday?

A Sure. _____, Mr. Montoya.

Boris works at the Copy Shop. Fill in his schedule for next week.
Use the times below.

Copy Shop

Schedule for week of _____ to _____

Monday 9:00 - 5:00	Tuesday	Wednesday
Thursday	**Friday**	**Saturday**

Monday 9:00-5:00	Tuesday 10:30-6:30	Wednesday 8:30-5:30
Thursday 9:00-5:00	Friday 8:30-5:30	

6A. COMPLETE

Complete the dialogs with *can* and *can't*

Can	I you he she we they	leave work early today?

Yes, No,	I you he she we they	can. can't.

1. **A** ___Can___ I leave work early next Friday?

   B No, I'm sorry. You _____ .

2. **A** Anton, _____ you work for me next Saturday? I have an appointment.

   B Sure, I _____ do that. _____ you work for me on Monday?

   A No problem.

3. **A** Sara, _____ you stay late on Tuesday? We need some extra help.

   B No, I'm sorry, I _____ . I have a class. But I _____ come in early.

   A Great. Thanks.

4. **A** _____ you help me with this copier?

   B Yes, I _____ .

Unit 4

Read Marty's time card. Answer the questions.

TIME CARD

· ·

Fill in each day completely.

Name: __Marty Kelly__

Day: __Monday__   Date: __January 15, 1999__

Time In: __4:15__   Time Out: _____

What	time	is it?
	month	
	day	
	year	

It's	7:45.
	January.
	Tuesday.
	2001.

1. What day is it? _____ Monday _____

2. What month is it? _____

3. What year is it? _____

Look at Marty's time card again. Complete the questions.
Write the answers.

Is it	Tuesday?
	July 15?
	3:00?
	Memorial Day?

Yes,	it	is.
No,		isn't.

1. ____Is it____ Monday? _____ Yes, it is. _____

2. _____ March? _____

3. _____ July 15? _____

4. _____ the year 2000? _____

Unit 4

Read the schedule. Circle the answers.

WARREN MANUFACTURING

First Shift – 7:00 to 3:00
Second Shift – 3:00 to 11:00

Name	Sunday 4/15	Monday 4/16	Tuesday 4/17	Wednesday 4/18	Thursday 4/19	Friday 4/20	Saturday 4/21
Olga Klonsky Second shift	off	3:00-11:00	3:00-11:00	1:00-11:00	3:00-11:00	3:00-11:00	off
Regular hours		8	8	8	8	8	
Overtime hours				2			
Maya Larsen Second shift	3:00-11:00	3:00-11:00	2:00-12:00	1:00-11:00	3:00-11:00	off	off
Regular hours	8	8	8	8	8		
Overtime hours			2	2			
Kevin Poulin First shift	7:00-3:00	7:00-3:00	6:00-4:00	7:00-3:00	off	7:00-3:00	off
Regular hours	8	8	8	8		8	
Overtime hours			2	1		1	

1. Which shift does Kevin work?   (first)   second

2. How many hours overtime does Maya have?   0   4

3. Does Olga have Monday off?   yes   no

4. Who has Thursday off?   Kevin   Maya

Kevin wants to take Friday off. Who can he ask to work for him?

_____

Unit 4

Read the ad. You just got this job at Bayside Industries. Fill out your schedule with the times and days you work.

DELIVERY DRIVER NEEDED
Bayside Industries is looking for an experienced driver who can work from 10 at night to 6 in the morning on Monday and Tuesday, 6 at night to 2 in the morning on Thursday and Friday, and 3 in the afternoon to 11 at night on Saturday. Call 555-4546.

Schedule for week of _____.	
Sunday	
Monday	
Tuesday	
Wednesday	
Thursday	
Friday	
Saturday	
Total hours worked: _____	

1. You need to go to the doctor. What's a good day and time

   for the appointment? _____

2. Your friend wants to go to a movie with you.

   What day(s) can you go? _____

3. What days do you have off? _____

7C. CHECK

Your supervisor wants you to prepare the schedule for your work group. Put a check (✔) by the information you need to know.

___✔___ 1. the number of shifts each day

_____ 2. the number of people for each shift

_____ 3. days each person can work

_____ 4. hours each person can work

_____ 5. overtime each person can work

Can you think of anything else you need to know to write a work schedule?

_____

8. REQUEST TIME OFF

Make a list of five reasons you might need time off.

1. _____

2. _____

3. _____

4. _____

5. _____

Fill out the form. Use one of the reasons from your list.

Request for Time Off

Name: _____

Today's date: _____

Day and date you would like off: _____

No. of hours you would like off: _____

Explanation: _____

_____

_____   _____
Supervisor's Approval   Date

9. THINK ABOUT YOUR LEARNING

Check the skills you learned in this unit.

❑ **1.** Read, write, and say times, days, and dates

❑ **2.** Interpret work schedules

❑ **3.** Ask to change your work hours

❑ **4.** Respond to requests to change your schedule

Look at the skills you checked.
Which ones can help you at work? Write the numbers. _____

Unit 4

Customer Service

1A. WRITE

Is this good customer service? Look at each picture. Write *yes* or *no*.

1. __yes__

2. _____

3. _____

4. _____

1B. CIRCLE

Did you write *no* for two pictures in 1A? Why? Circle the letter of each sentence that tells what's wrong with the customer service.

a. They're helping the customer.

b. The customer is waiting.

c. They're greeting the customer.

d. They aren't talking to the customer.

Complete each greeting. Choose the best word. Write it on the line.

| Welcome | Thank you | ~~help~~ | may |

1. Can I _____ *help* _____ you?

2. Hello, _____
I take your order?

3. _____ for calling Star Computers.

4. _____ to the Desert Inn. Can I show you to your room?

2B. WRITE

Think about customers you greet. Or think about people who greet you as a customer. Write two good ways to greet a customer.

1. _____

2. _____

Unit 5

Look at each picture. What would you say to give good customer service?
Write the letter in the circle.

 c

 ◯

 ◯

a. Would you like a refund?

b. May I get you some coffee?

✗ The mail room is down the hall on the right.

4. WRITE

Complete the dialog. Apologize to the customer. Write the best word.

A Good afternoon, can I help you?

B Yes, I'd like to return this radio.

A Sure, what's the ____problem____?

B It isn't working.

A I'm _____. Would you like

a _____ or an exchange?

B A refund, please.

A _____. Please accept our _____.

~~problem~~

sorry

apology

refund

Sure

Unit 5

Norma Valdez is a customer at the Supply Warehouse. Complete her order.

1. Norma wants 3 gallons of paint.

2. Norma wants 10 boxes of nails.

3. Norma wants 2 paintbrushes.

SUPPLY WAREHOUSE Date: _3/15/99_ Order #: _A5-56734_ Name:_____

Qty.	Description	Price for each	Total
3	*gallons of paint*	$7.95	$23.85

6A. WRITE

Complete the dialog. Write *a/an* or *some*.

I need	a	tube of glue.
	an	electric drill.
	some	nails and screws.

I need	some	glue.
		paint.

A Hello, can I help you?

B Yes, please. I need some supplies. First, _____*some*_____ tape. I'd like

_____ large roll. Also _____ extension cord and

_____ envelopes.

A We have _____ box of small envelopes for $2.95.

B OK, then I need _____ electric stapler.

A No problem.

How	much	gas	do you want?
		oil	
	many	gallons of gas	
		batteries	

Write each item under the correct question.

paint	clocks	nails	cameras
photocopies	oil	light bulbs	juice
coffee	spark plugs	paper	money

How much?	How many?
paint	

6C. WRITE

You work in the warehouse of Superior Electrical Supply.
Ask questions to fill the order.

A Here's Jeff Wilson's order. First, he needs switches.

B _____How many_____ switches?

A Six. He also wants extension cords.

B _____ extension cords?

A Three long and one short. He also wants some electrical tape.

B _____ tape?

A Four rolls. He needs some light bulbs, too.

B _____ light bulbs?

A Just one box of six. That's it. Let's send the order out.

Unit 5

Read the customer service policy for Bargain Office Supply.
Answer the questions. Write *yes* or *no*.

BARGAIN OFFICE SUPPLY

1. All items can be returned for a full refund or exchange if the customer has the receipt.

2. If the customer does not have the receipt, items may be returned for a store credit.

3. There are no refunds or exchanges for items the customer breaks.

Our Customer Service Department is open
8:00 to 6:00 Monday through Saturday
Call 555-5676

---

1. Sandra bought a clock on Tuesday, but she doesn't like it. She has the receipt.
   Can she return the clock? __yes__

2. Boris bought a calculator for $59.95. The calculator doesn't work.
   He still has his receipt. Can he get his money back? _____

3. Sara has a question about some supplies she bought. It is 5:00 on
   Sunday afternoon. Can she call the Customer Service Department? _____

4. Joe wants to return the coffee maker he bought last week.
   He doesn't have his receipt. Can he get a store credit? _____

Do you help customers? What do you do if a customer isn't happy?

_____

What can you do if you are an unhappy customer?

_____

You work in the maintenance department of the Tiptop Company. You notice these problems in the building. Write the letter for the sentence that says what's wrong.

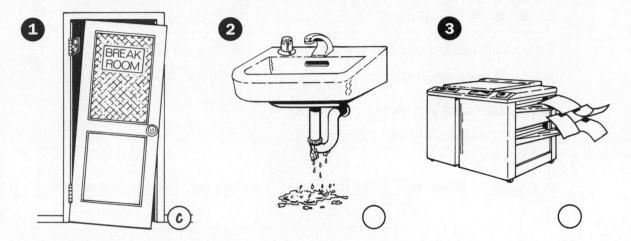

a. There's a leak in the men's room.

b. Paper is coming out of the copier in the mail room.

~~**c.**~~ The door to the break room is broken.

7C. WRITE

Fill out the maintenance request form for the problems in 7B.

Maintenance Request ✦Tiptop Company

Name: _____

Department: _____ Date: _____

Problem: _____

_____

Problem: _____

_____

Problem: _____

_____

Please describe each problem. All repairs will be made within two days of receiving the request.

Look at the checklist. Circle *yes* or *no*.

Cars Unlimited
✦ ✦ ✦ ✦ ✦ ✦ **Car Rental**　　　**How are we doing?**

Please complete the following checklist and tell us how we can serve you better.

Name: _Delores Martin_　　　　　　　　　　Date: _3/13/99_

☑ **The rental clerk was friendly and efficient.**

❏ **The car was ready when I arrived.**

❏ **The car was clean.**

Comments: _I had to wait about 15 minutes to get my car. The car was not clean._

1. Ms. Martin is a satisfied customer.　　yes　(no)

2. The car was clean when Ms. Martin picked it up.　　yes　　no

3. The rental clerk was friendly.　　yes　　no

What can you do about Ms. Martin's complaint? How can you keep her as a customer? Circle numbers of the best answers.

1. Apologize to Ms. Martin

2. Don't talk to Ms. Martin

3. Give Ms. Martin a refund

9. THINK ABOUT YOUR LEARNING

Check the skills you learned in this unit.

❏ 1. Greet customers

❏ 2. Give good customer service

❏ 3. Understand commitments to customers

❏ 4. Respond to customers' complaints

Look at the skills you checked.
Which ones can help you at work? Write the numbers. _____

1A. WRITE

Look at the picture. Answer the questions.

1. Where does she work? _____ **Quality Car Rental** _____

2. What time does it open? _____

3. Is she on time? _____

4. Is she dressed appropriately? _____

5. Is she following the rules? _____

1B. WRITE

Write about your workplace or school.

1. What time does your job or school open? _____

2. Do you get there on time? _____

3. Are there rules about how to dress? _____

4. Are there rules for calling in sick? _____

Read the question. Circle what the person wears to work.

1. Which person wears a hat?

   (bus driver)   waiter   sales assistant

2. Which person wears work boots?

   secretary   cashier   machinist

3. Which person wears coveralls?

   mechanic   waiter   store manager

4. Which person wears a sweatshirt?

   sales assistant   truck driver   secretary

2B. WRITE

Are the people dressed appropriately for work? Write *yes* or *no*.

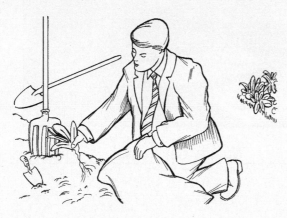

1. __no__

2. _____

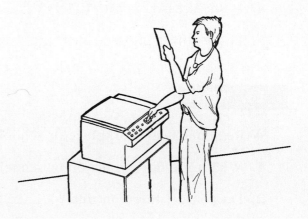

3. _____

4. _____

Write what you wear to work or school. _____

Unit 6

Complete the dialogs.

| Excuse me | Thank you | Ms. | Certainly |

1. **A** ___Excuse me___ . When does the second shift start?

   B 11:00.

2. **A** Ricardo, can you help me?

   B _____ . What do you need?

3. **A** Dennis, you're doing a good job.

   B _____ , Mr. Jones.

4. **A** Dawn, can you work overtime on Thursday?

   B Of course, _____ Valdez.

4. CHOOSE

Write the letter of the rule each worker is following.

a. Clock in by 8:30.

b. Wear work boots.

c. Call your supervisor by 8:00 when you're sick.

d. Wear a hard hat.

Unit 6

5. CIRCLE

Read the rules. What should the employees do? Circle the letter.

1. Stella is sick.

   (a.) Call her supervisor

   b. Just stay home

2. Alex goes to lunch.

   a. Clock out

   b. Clock out and in

3. Anita is late for work.

   a. Not say anything

   b. Talk to her supervisor

Company Rules

1. Wear your name tag.

2. Call your supervisor when you are sick.

3. Talk to your supervisor if you are late.

4. Clock out and in for lunch breaks.

6A. WRITE

Look at the picture. Complete the dialog. Write *this*, *that*, *these*, or *those*.

| Please take | this | memo to customer service. |
| | that | |

| Please fill | these | boxes. |
| | those | |

A We need to move _____this_____ paper over there.

B OK, what about _____ boxes?

A We can leave _____ boxes where they are. But we need to

move _____ toner cartridges to the room down the hall.

Unit 6

Write the form of the word.

What	time	do	I	stop?
			we	
			you	
			they	
		does	he	
			she	
			it	

I	stop	at 3:15.
We		
You		
They		
He	stops	
She		
It		

A What time _____*does*_____ the second shift _____*start*_____ (**start**)?

B It _____ (**start**) at 11:00.

A Which shift _____ Kara _____ (**work**)?

B She _____ (**work**) the second shift. What about you?

What time _____ you _____ (**leave**)?

A I _____ (**leave**) at 9:30.

Write the form of the word.

Do	I	speak to the manager?
	we	
	you	
	they	
Does	he	
	she	

| Yes, | I | do. |
| | she | does. |

| No, | I | don't. |
| | he | doesn't. |

1. **A** _____*Does*_____ Antonio _____*walk*_____ (**walk**) to work?

   B No, he _*doesn't*_____ .

2. **A** _____ the students _____ (**come**) to class every day?

   B Yes, they _____ .

3. **A** _____ the restaurant _____ (**open**) at 6:00?

   B Yes, it _____ .

4. **A** _____ you _____ (**work**) on Mondays?

   B _____ I _____ .

Unit 6

Read the job evaluation. Read the questions. Circle the answers.

Name: <u>Sylvia Montero</u>   Position: <u>cashier</u>   Date: <u>7/17/99</u>

Circle the word that best describes the employee's performance.

1. The employee is punctual. He/She arrives at work on time.

   very good   (good)   poor

2. The employee is helpful. He/She helps other employees.

   (very good)   good   poor

3. The employee dresses appropriately. He/She always wears the proper clothes and equipment.

   very good   good   (poor)

4. The employee is polite. He/She is polite and pleasant to supervisors, coworkers, and customers.

   very good   (good)   poor

5. The employee is flexible. He/She is willing to do different tasks.

   (very good)   good   poor

Comments: <u>Sylvia is a good employee. She is always helpful to other employees. She usually arrives on time. But Sylvia sometimes forgets her cash register key.</u>

1. What does Sylvia do?   welder   (cashier)

2. Does Sylvia arrive at work on time?   usually   never

3. Is Sylvia helpful?   yes   no

4. Is Sylvia polite?   yes   no

5. What does Sylvia sometimes forget?   coveralls   key

Do you think Sylvia is a good employee? _____
Why? Give two reasons.

_____

_____

What can she do to improve her work?

_____

7B. CHECK

Answer the questions. Check *yes* or *no*.

Yes No

❑ ❑ **1.** Do you usually arrive at work or school on time?

❑ ❑ **2.** Do you dress appropriately for work or school?

❑ ❑ **3.** Are you polite to your coworkers, supervisors, and customers?

❑ ❑ **4.** Do you try to help your coworkers?

❑ ❑ **5.** Are you willing to do different tasks when your supervisor asks?

7C. WRITE

Look at the answers you checked in 7B. Can you improve something?
Write the numbers of the questions you can improve. _____

How can you improve your work? Write one or two ideas.

_____

_____

8A. CHOOSE

Read the question. Choose the answer that is polite. Circle the letter.

1. Ricardo, can you help me move these boxes, please?

   a. No.

   (b.) No, I'm sorry. I can help you later.

2. Marta, could you work for me next Tuesday?

   a. No problem. I'd be happy to.

   b. Yeah.

3. Ana, please take these invoices to shipping.

   a. Do I have to do it right now?

   b. Sure. I'll do it right away.

Unit 6

Write a polite answer.

1. A John, can you work late on Friday night?

B _____ *Sure, I can do that.* _____

2. A Ms. Valdez, can I speak to you?

B _____

3. A Ricardo, can you help me move those boxes to the meeting room?

B _____

Think about your workplace or school. Write a request.
Then write a polite answer.

A _____

B _____

9. THINK ABOUT YOUR LEARNING

Check the skills you learned in this unit.

❏ 1. Follow company rules

❏ 2. Call in sick

❏ 3. Use polite language

❏ 4. Improve your performance

Look at the skills you checked.
Which ones can help you at work? Write the numbers. _____

1A. WRITE

Complete the sentences about Maria.

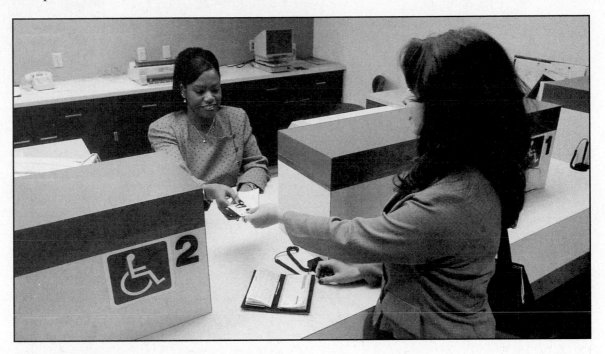

| bank | paycheck | money | deposit |

1. Maria is at the _____**bank**_____ .

2. Banks handle _____ .

3. Maria takes her _____ to the bank.

4. She makes a _____ each Friday.

1B. WRITE

Answer the question. Write *yes* or *no*.

1. Do you use a bank? _____

2. Do you handle money at work? _____

3. Do you fill out a time card? _____

4. Do you get a paycheck each week? _____

2A. MATCH

Match the amount of money with the picture. Write the letter.

 a

 b

 c

 d

 e

✖ f

1. $35.36 ___f___   **2.** $27.55 _____   **3.** $ 2.75 _____

4. $14.35 _____   **5.** $ 7.61 _____   **6.** $10.07 _____

2B. COUNT

Look at the picture. Write the amount of money.

1. ___**$30.55**___

2. _____

3. _____

4. _____

Unit 7

Answer the questions about Laura's time card. Circle *yes* or *no*.

ALL CITY GLASS COMPANY

Day	Sunday	Monday	Tuesday	Wednesday	Thursday	Friday	Saturday
in	—	12:30	9:00	9:30	—	12:30	10:00
out	—	8:30	7:00	6:30	—	8:30	7:00
Hours	0	8	10	9	0	8	9

Total Hours __44__ Hourly Rate __$6.75__ Total Pay __$297.00__

Employee Signature *Laura Vargas*   Date __2/21/99__

1. Does Laura work more than 40 hours this week?   (yes)   no

2. Is Laura's hourly rate $6.75?   yes   no

3. Does Laura work 8 hours on Wednesday?   yes   no

4. Is Laura's total pay correct?   yes   no

Do you fill out a time card at work? What information do you fill out?
For example, do you put the date? Write two things you put on
your time card. _____

Number the parts of the deposit slip.

~~1.~~ date   **2.** name

3. amount of cash to deposit   **4.** total amount of deposit

Complete the deposit slip. Deposit your paycheck of $325.45.

DEPOSIT SLIP

NAME _____

ADDRESS _____

_____

DATE _____
Deposits may not be available for immediate withdrawal.

_____
Sign here for cash received (if required).

eagle savings bank
Medina, CA

	CASH		
CHECKS			
CHECK TOTAL			
SUB-TOTAL			
LESS CASH RECEIVED			

$

---

5. WRITE

You work at Office Cleaners, Inc. Fill in the check.
Pay Crystal Cleaning Supply $69.45.

OCI **Office Cleaners Inc.**
45 Central Avenue
Miami, FL 33172

2315

PAY TO THE
ORDER OF _____ $ _____

_____ DOLLARS

★ STATE SAVINGS BANK
Miami, FL

FOR _____ _____

6A. WRITE

Write the question. Complete the answer.

How many	checks	are there?

There's	a check.
There are	checks.

1. ___**How many bills are there?**___   ___**There are**___ four bills.

2. _____   _____ one time card.

3. _____   _____ six paychecks.

Unit 7

Luis is a new employee at City Cleaners. Complete the questions and answers.

Is	there	a W-4 tax form?	Yes,	there	is.	No,	there	isn't.
Are		tax forms?			are.			aren't.

A _____ *Are there* _____ forms for Luis to fill out?

B Yes, _____ *there are* _____. Give him these forms, please.

A _____ a place to punch in every day?

B No, _____. City Cleaners doesn't use a time clock.

A _____ a break room for employees?

B Yes, _____. It's down the hall next to the office.

Look at the check register. Write questions using *which*.

Which	line do I sign my name on?
	space is for checks?

Check Number	Date	Description	Amount of Withdrawal (−)	Amount of Deposit (+)	Balance	
					657	98
4356	2/13	Bay State Cleaning Service	56	93	56	93
					601	05
4357	2/14	Restaurant Suppliers	95	50	95	50
					505	55
4358	2/15	The Flower Market	47	23	47	23
					458	32

1. _____ *Which check is for Restaurant Suppliers?* _____
   Check number 4357 is for Restaurant Suppliers.

2. _____
   Check number 4356 is for $56.93.

3. _____
   Check number 4358 is from 2/15.

Unit 7

Read Mark's time card for this week. Answer the questions.

TIME CARD

Antonio's Restaurant

Week Ending 8/21/99

Employee Signature _Mark Jones_   Social Security No. 000-55-5534

	Sunday	Monday	Tuesday	Wednesday	Thursday	Friday	Saturday
Start	11:00	5:00	off	11:00	off	3:00	2:00
Finish	5:00	12:30		3:00		11:00	12:00
Hours	6	7½	0	4	0	8	10

Total Hours 35½   Pay Rate $5.55 per hour _____

Supervisor's Signature

1. Mark doesn't work on which days? _____ Tuesday, Thursday _____

2. Who signs the time card? _____

3. How much does Mark make an hour? _____

4. What time does Mark begin work on Friday? _____

5. What time does Mark finish work on Saturday? _____

6. How many hours does Mark work on Wednesday? _____

7. What are Mark's total hours for the week? _____

Fill in your own information on the time card. Figure out the number of hours you work or go to school each day and each week. Write in your total hours for this week or last week.

TIME CARD

Week Ending _____

Employee Signature _____   Social Security No. _____

	Sunday	Monday	Tuesday	Wednesday	Thursday	Friday	Saturday
Start							
Finish							
Hours							

Total Hours _____ Pay Rate _____ per hour _____

Supervisor's Signature

You are the manager at Antonio's Restaurant. Alex Brown is a new employee.
Help him fill out his time card. Use the information below.

Alex has Tuesday and Wednesday off. He works from 11:00 to 7:00 on
Monday and Thursday, 1:00 to 9:00 on Friday, and 10:00 to 8:00 on Saturday.
He makes $5.20 an hour. His social security number is 000-31-4323.

Antonio's Restaurant

TIME CARD

Week Ending _____

Employee Signature _____ Social Security No. _____

	Sunday	Monday	Tuesday	Wednesday	Thursday	Friday	Saturday
Start							
Finish							
Hours							

Total Hours _____ Pay Rate _____ per hour _____
Supervisor's Signature

Look at the time card. How much should Alex's paycheck be? _____

Is his paycheck correct? _____ Sign the check if it is correct.

Antonio's Restaurant

Pier 44
San Francisco, CA

Bank of California
San Francisco, CA

NO. 4356

PAY TO THE
ORDER OF

DATE 07/25/99

TWO HUNDRED AND TWO DOLLARS AND EIGHTY CENTS

NOT GOOD AFTER 60 DAYS FROM DATE ISSUED

PAY THIS AMOUNT
***202.80

2700 20 526

Signature

Look at the W-4 form. Write the number of the line where you fill in the information.

Form **W-4** Department of the Treasury Internal Revenue Service	**Employee's Withholding Allowance Certificate** ▶ **For Privacy Act and Paperwork Reduction Act Notice, see reverse.**	OMB No. 1545-0010

1 Type or print your first name and middle initial	Last name	2 Your social security number
Home address (number and street or rural route)	3 ☐ Single ☐ Married ☐ Married, but withhold at higher Single rate. **Note:** *If married, but legally separated, or spouse is a nonresident alien, check the Single box.*	
City or town, state, and ZIP code	4 If your last name differs from that on your social security card, check here and call 1-800-772-1213 for a new card . . . . . ▶ ☐	

5 Total number of allowances you are claiming (from line G above or from the worksheets on page 2 if they apply) . **5**

6 Additional amount, if any, you want withheld from each paycheck . . . . **6** $

7 I claim exemption from withholding for (year) and I certify that I meet **BOTH** of the following conditions for exemption:
 • Last year I had a right to a refund of **ALL** Federal income tax withheld because I had **NO** tax liability; **AND**
 • This year I expect a refund of **ALL** Federal income tax withheld because I expect to have **NO** tax liability.
 If you meet both conditions, enter "EXEMPT" here . . . . ▶ **7**

Under penalties of perjury, I certify that I am entitled to the number of withholding allowances claimed on this certificate or entitled to claim exempt status.

Employee's signature ▶   Date ▶

8 Employer's name and address (Employer: Complete 8 and 10 only if sending to the IRS)	9 Office code (optional)	10 Employer identification number

Cat. No. 10220Q

a. name ____1____

b. married or single _____

c. total number of allowances _____

d. social security number _____

Now fill out the W-4 form with information about you.

Check the skills you learned in this unit.

❏ **1.** Count money

❏ **2.** Fill out a time card

❏ **3.** Make a deposit

❏ **4.** Understand a W-4 form

Look at the skills you checked.
Which ones can help you at work? Write the numbers. _____

1A. MATCH

Look at the pictures. What safety equipment are the people wearing?
Write the letter or letters on the line.

1. _b,d_   2. _____   3. _____   4. _____

(a) hard hat   (b) gloves   (c) work boots   (d) safety glasses

1B. MATCH

Match the worker and the sign. Write the letters.

1. _____   2. _____

(a) **EMPLOYEES** _MUST_ **WASH HANDS BEFORE RETURNING TO WORK**

(b) **GLOVES REQUIRED IN THIS AREA**

(c) **DANGER HARD HAT AREA**

Write the names of the parts of the body.

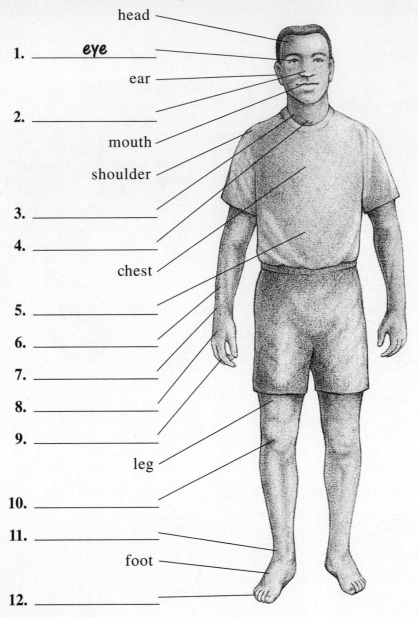

head

1. ___*eye*___

ear

2. _____

mouth

shoulder

3. _____

4. _____

chest

5. _____

6. _____

7. _____

8. _____

9. _____

leg

10. _____

11. _____

foot

12. _____

ankle
arm
~~eye~~
finger
hand
knee
neck
nose
stomach
throat
toe
wrist

2B. WRITE

What part of the body is the equipment for? Complete the chart.

safety glasses	*eyes*
work boots	
gloves	
hard hat	

Unit 8

A car is on fire in front of your home. Write what you say to the 911 operator.

911: 911 operator. What's your name and phone number?

You: _____

911: What's the emergency?

You: _____

911: We'll send help right away. What's the address?

You: _____

4. COMPLETE

What's wrong? Complete the sentences.

~~burn~~ sick
broken leg stomachache

1. He has a _____burn_____ .

2. They feel _____ .

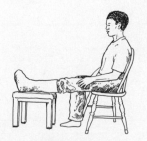

3. He has a _____ .

4. She has a _____ .

Unit 8

59

5. CIRCLE

Who do you call? Read the sentence. Circle the letter.

1. The doctor's office across the street is on fire.

(a.)   b.   c.

2. Marcos got some windshield washer fluid in his eye.

a.   b.   c.

3. Look! Smoke is coming out of the copier in the manager's office.

a.   b.   c.

4. Sara cut her hand. It's bleeding a lot.

a.   b.   c.

6A. WRITE

How do they feel? Complete the dialogs.

How	do	I we you they	feel?
	does	he she it	

I We You They	feel	fine.
He She It	feels	

1. A How ____*do*____ you ____*feel*____?

   B I ____*feel*____ sick.

2. A How _____ they _____?

   B They _____ happy.

3. A How _____ she _____?

   B She _____ nervous.

Unit 8

Write sentences with *have* or *has* and the words in the box.

I We You They	have	the flu.
She He	has	

broken arms   fever   headache   stomachaches

1. She _____ **has a headache** _____ .   **2.** He _____ .

3. They _____ .   **4.** We _____ .

Complete the sentences. Use *have*, *has*, *feel*, or *feels*.

A Hi, Victor. How are you?

B I _____ *feel* _____ fine, but Galena _____ the flu.

She _____ a fever and her head hurts.

A That's too bad.

B What about you? How are you and Natalie?

A We _____ fine, but our manager is sick. She _____

the flu, too.

Unit 8

Match the sign with the workplace. Write the letter.

a

b

c

d

e

f

1. _c_

2. _____

3. _____

4. _____

Unit 8

What's the matter? Look at the picture. Complete the sentence.

1. They're not wearing __*work boots*__.

2. She's not wearing _____.

3. The floor is _____.

4. He's not wearing a _____.

Unit 8

Read the safety procedures. Then read the sentences. Do the people follow the safety procedures? Circle *yes* or *no*.

Fire Procedures

1. When you hear the fire alarm, go to the nearest exit. Leave the building quickly.
2. Do not stop to get your things.
3. Walk. Do not run.
4. Use the stairs. Do not use the elevator.
5. Meet your supervisor in parking lot B.
6. Stay outside. Do not return to the building.
7. Follow instructions from your supervisor and the fire fighters.

1. Nora leaves the building immediately.   (yes)   no
2. Joe goes to his work station to get his hat.   yes   no
3. Ricardo looks for his supervisor in parking lot B.   yes   no
4. Tim takes the elevator.   yes   no
5. Sonia runs to the nearest exit.   yes   no

9. THINK ABOUT YOUR LEARNING

Check the skills you learned in this unit.

❏ 1. Identify parts of the body

❏ 2. Handle an emergency

❏ 3. Describe injuries and illnesses

❏ 4. Read safety signs

❏ 5. Follow safety instructions

Look at the skills you checked.

Which ones can help you at work? Write the numbers. _____

1A. CIRCLE

Look at the picture. Read the question. Circle the answer.

1. Is Mr. Marcos showing Ana how to do something?　(yes)　no

2. Are they working together or alone?　together　alone

3. Where do they work?　a mailroom　a kitchen　an auto parts store

1B. CHECK

Put a check (✔) by the things you do at work or school.

_____ I usually work alone.

_____ I usually work with other people.

_____ I show someone how to do a job.

_____ Someone shows me how to do a job.

Unit 9

Match the picture with the job duty. Write three letters for each job.

1. waitress: _c_ _____   2. hotel housekeeper: _____

a. **clean rooms**

b. **count money**

~~c.~~ **make coffee**

d. **make change**

e. **take customers' orders**

f. **put soap and towels in rooms**

g. **use the vacuum cleaner**

h. **use the cash register**

i. **bring food to customers**

3. cashier: _____

Write the name of your job or a job you are interested in. Write three job duties for the job.

Job: _____

Duties: _____

_____

_____

3A. CIRCLE

John didn't do a very good job. His supervisor is talking to him.
What can John say to the supervisor? Circle the letters.

(a.) I'm sorry.

b. You're wrong about that.

c. Oh, no. I'll try to do it right next time.

d. Please show me the correct way to do it.

e. That's your problem.

f. My shift is over now. I want to go home.

g. What are you talking about?

h. You're right. I need to be careful.

3B. MATCH

What does the supervisor tell the employees? Write the letter.

a. Marla, the table looks beautiful.

b. Fred, please try to be more careful.

c. Chen, you need to get to work on time every day.

3C. WRITE

What do the employees in 3B say to their bosses? Write their answers.

1. Chen: _____

2. Marla: _____

3. Fred: _____

Unit 9

What skills does the worker need? Circle the letters.

1. truck driver

   (a.) drives carefully

   b. likes to talk to people

   (c.) has a commercial
      driver's license

2. data entry clerk

   a. likes to type

   b. can use a computer

   c. enjoys working
      with children

3. security guard

   a. knows how to
      fix cars

   b. likes to keep
      people safe

   c. enjoys watching
      people

5A. WRITE

Read what the supervisors say. Are they happy with the employees' work?
Write *yes* or *no*.

yes   **1.** Leon, you're really friendly to the customers.
           I like the way you smile and say hello to them.

_____   **2.** Marty, you sometimes forget to water these flowers.
           Please water them every day.

_____   **3.** Rosa, this car looks great. It's really clean inside.

_____   **4.** Lin, this floor doesn't look very clean. You need to vacuum it again.

_____   **5.** Chris, you're here early every morning. You're never late.

5B. WRITE

Think of a time your supervisor or teacher was happy with your work.
What did the person say? Write a few words.

_____

Complete the sentences. Write about yourself.
Use *always*, *usually*, *sometimes*, or *never*.

always	100%	I always arrive at work on time.
usually	↑	
sometimes	↓	
never	0%	I usually work at the warehouse on Tuesdays.

1. I _____ sometimes _____ arrive at work early.

2. I _____ work with customers.

3. I _____ work on Saturdays.

4. I _____ help others at work.

5. I _____ work overtime.

Complete the sentences.

| I always keep my work area clean. | I'm cleaning my work area now. |

1. **a.** Today Anton _____ is working _____ (**work**) the second shift.

   b. Anton usually _____ works _____ (**work**) the first shift.

2. **a.** I sometimes _____ (**take**) training classes at work.

   b. Right now I _____ (**learn**) data entry.

3. **a.** Sylvia always _____ (**train**) new employees.

   b. Right now, Sylvia _____ (**teach**) them how to use the cash register.

4. **a.** You and I usually _____ (**drive**) to work together.

   b. We _____ (**take**) your car now because my car is in the repair shop.

What do you do every day? What are you doing now? Write two sentences.

_____

_____

Unit 9   69

7A. READ AND CIRCLE

Read the training manual.

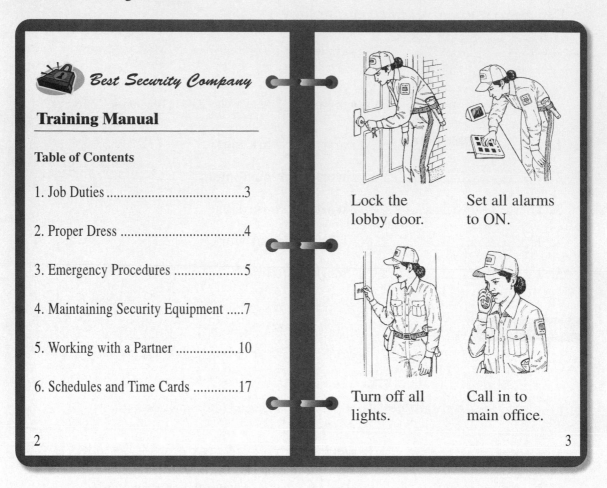

Best Security Company

Training Manual

Table of Contents

2

Lock the lobby door.

Set all alarms to ON.

Turn off all lights.

Call in to main office.

3

Read the question. Circle the answer.

1. Who is this training manual for?

   truck drivers   (security guards)   waiters and waitresses

2. Is calling customers one of the duties?   yes   no

3. Does the manual tell employees how to dress?   yes   no

4. What page tells what to do in a fire?   5   10   13

5. Should employees turn off the alarms?   yes   no

6. Should employees turn off the lights?   yes   no

7. Which chapter tells employees about filling out time cards?   1   5   6

8. Do the security guards sometimes work with a partner?   yes   no

You're a new employee at Best Security Company. Look at the training manual. Write a checklist for getting ready for work.

Best Security Company

Proper Dress

Here is the uniform that our guards wear every day.

hat

black shirt

name tag

black pants

black shoes

4

1.   hat

2. _____

3. _____

4. _____

5. _____

7C. WRITE

Write a checklist for getting ready for your work or school.

1. _____

2. _____

3. _____

8. WRITE

Tim wants to evaluate his work. He writes these sentences.

What I'm Good At

_____ I always arrive on time. _____

What I Need to Improve

_____ I need to keep my work area clean. _____

Evaluate your work. Write sentences. Use the phrases to help you.

arrive on time	learn different tasks
dress appropriately	finish work on time
help my coworkers	help customers

What I'm Good At

1. _____

2. _____

3. _____

4. _____

What I Need to Improve

1. _____

2. _____

3. _____

9. THINK ABOUT YOUR LEARNING

Check the skills you learned in this unit.

❏ 1. Give and receive feedback

❏ 2. Talk about job duties

❏ 3. Evaluate my work

❏ 4. Identify job skills

Look at the skills you checked.
Which ones can help you at work? Write the numbers. _____

Unit 9

UNIT 10 ▸ Career Development

1. CIRCLE

Look at the pictures. Answer the questions. Circle the letter.

1. What's she doing?

   (a.) She's filling out a job application.

   b. She's reading the newspaper.

2. Where do you think she wants to work?

   a. She wants to work in an office.

   b. She wants to work in a restaurant.

3. What's he doing?

   a. He's looking for a job.

   b. He's working.

4. Where is he?

   a. He's at home.

   b. He's visiting a human resources department.

What are two other ways to find a job?

_____   _____

2A. WRITE

Look at the picture. Write the people's jobs.

| cashier | cook | delivery driver | police officer | ~~waiter~~ | waitress |

1. _____ waiter _____

2. _____

3. _____

4. _____

5. _____

6. _____

2B. MATCH

Match the skill with the job. Write the letter.

___e___ 1. delivery driver   **a.** use a saw

_____ 2. grocery clerk   **b.** take care of children

_____ 3. construction worker   **c.** prepare food

_____ 4. bus driver   **d.** put food on shelves

_____ 5. cook   ~~**e.**~~ drive a truck

_____ 6. child care worker   **f.** drive a bus

Unit 10

3. WRITE

Complete the dialog. Write the words.

bus	cook	doing	looking	~~studying~~

A Dave, how's school?

B Great, Jean. I'm _____studying_____ cooking.

I want to be a _____ in a restaurant.

And you? What are you _____ these days?

A I'm _____ for a job. I want to be

a _____ driver.

B Well, good luck.

What are you doing these days? Write one or two sentences.

_____

_____

4. CIRCLE

Look at each person's skills and experience. Circle the best job for each person.

1. Luis
√ He was a nurse in his country.
√ He knows first aid.

  receptionist   (medical technician)

2. Victor
√ He was a carpenter in his country.
√ He can use a table saw.

  painter   carpenter's helper

3. Sabrina
√ She was a cook in a nice restaurant.
√ She likes to prepare food.

  teacher's aide   baker

4. Marta
√ She likes to take care of trees.
√ She can use lawn mowers.

  delivery driver   gardener

Unit 10

5. CHECK

Look at Ed's job experience and training. Check the things he can do for work.

Name:	Ed Johnson
Job Experience:	3 years as construction supervisor
Education and Training:	high school diploma
	training classes for carpenters at City Technical School

__✔__ build a house   _____ use tools   _____ fix a car

_____ bake cakes   _____ supervise workers   _____ clean rooms

6A. WRITE

Complete the dialog.

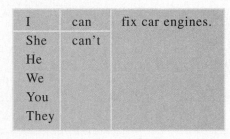

I	can	fix car engines.
She	can't	
He		
We		
You		
They		

Can	she	fix car engines?
	you	

Yes,	I	can.
No,		can't.

A   Hello, I'm looking for a job.

B   What _____ **can** _____ you do?

A   I _____ cook. I _____ clean rooms, too.

B   _____ you drive a van?

A   No, I _____ . But I _____ learn.

B   Great. Then I _____ help you find a job.

A   Thanks.

Unit 10

Complete the dialogs.

I	was	a sales clerk.
She		
He		
You	were	sales clerks.
We		
You		
They		

Was	he	a sales clerk?
Were	they	sales clerks?

Yes,	he	was.
No,		wasn't.

Yes,	they	were.
No,		weren't.

1. Pablo—truck driver

A _____ **Was Pablo a truck driver?** _____

B Yes, he _____ **was** _____ .

2. Hans and Marta—painters

A _____

B No, they _____ .

3. Sara—tailor

A _____

B No, she _____ .

4. You—mechanic

A _____

B _____ , I _____ .

Complete the dialog.

How long were you a cook?

From	1993	to	1997.
	May		August.

For	four years.
	three months.

A Ms. Valdez, _____ **how long** _____ were you a delivery driver?

B I _____ a delivery driver for three years.

From 1996 _____ 1999.

A And I see that you were a gardener. _____ were you a gardener?

B _____ one year. _____ 1995 to 1996.

Unit 10

Read the want ads.

a **Short Order Cook** Needed

3 2 years experience necessary.
Position available immediately

2 at **The Family Diner**. Requires
ability to cook and bake and

work fast. For an interview,

1 call 555-1923.

b **Child Care Workers** Needed
River City Day Care
Experience required. We prefer
people who **speak English and
Chinese or Spanish.** Call Anita
Marcos at 555-2646 for an
interview.

c WANTED: **DELIVERY DRIVER**
Requires at least **two years truck
or van driving experience, a
commercial driver's license** and
a clean record. Call **On Time
Deliveries,** 555-3250.

d HOUSEKEEPERS NEEDED
IMMEDIATELY
The **Flagship Hotel** is looking for
housekeepers. No experience
necessary. Must have **a high
school diploma and be in good
health**. Call Cindy Smith at
555-1212.

Number the parts of the ad.

1. the skills or training you need

2. the company

3. the name of the job

7B. MATCH

Where should the people apply? Write the phone number.

1. Bettina
She was a teacher's aide from
1996–1999. She likes taking
care of children.

555-2646

2. John
He has a commercial driver's license.
He was a driver at A-1 Trucking for
three years.

3. Maria
She completed two cooking courses
at the Community Learning Center.
She was a cook for 4 years.

4. Sonia
She enjoys keeping her house clean.
She was a housekeeper for 1 year.

Unit 10

7C. COMPLETE

Fill out the job application.

North American Corporation
9632 Ocean Drive, San Francisco, CA 94134
Application For Employment

Personal Information

Name _____

Address _____

_____

Telephone _____ Social Security Number _____

Work Experience

Job _____ Employer _____

How long were you at this job? _____

_____

Job _____ Employer _____

How long were you at this job? _____

_____

Read and Sign

The above information is true and correct.

_____   _____
Signature   Date

7D. WRITE

You are getting ready to apply for a job.
Read the interview questions. Write your answers.

1. Do you work well with others? Write why.

_____

2. Are you organized? Write one example.

_____

3. Describe your perfect job. Write one reason it's perfect for you.

_____

Unit 10

8. WRITE

Think about what you do at work, at school, and at home.
Make a list of your skills.

My Skills

_____   _____

_____   _____

_____   _____

Look at your list of skills. Then look at the list of jobs below.
Add jobs if you wish. Circle the jobs you can do.

bellhop	receptionist
cashier	sales assistant
child care worker	secretary
driver	security guard
grocery clerk	tailor
janitor	truck driver
machinist	waiter or waitress
mechanic	warehouse worker

_____   _____

9. THINK ABOUT YOUR LEARNING

Check the skills you learned in this unit.

❏ **1.** Describe my job skills

❏ **2.** Read help-wanted ads

❏ **3.** Figure out the best job for me

❏ **4.** Complete a job application

Look at the skills you checked.
Which ones can help you at work? Write the numbers. _____

Answer Key

UNIT 1

Exercise 1A (page 1)
1. yes
2. yes
3. yes
4. no
5. yes

Exercise 1B (page 1)
Many answers are possible. Share your answers with another learner or your teacher.

Exercise 2A (page 2)
1. c
2. a
3. b

Exercise 2B (page 2)
1. Korean, truck driver
2. Russian, waitress
3. Spanish, construction worker
4. *Many answers are possible. Share your answers with another learner or your teacher.*

Exercise 2C (page 2)
1. Kee: Korea, Korean, truck driver
2. Kara: Russia, Russian, waitress
3. Manuel: Mexico, Spanish, construction worker
4. *Many answers are possible. Share your answers with another learner or your teacher.*

Exercise 3 (page 3)
1. c
2. b
3. a

Exercise 4 (page 3)
A Hi
B nice
A meet, too, like
C nice
B from

Exercise 5 (page 4)
1. b
2. a
3. b

Exercise 6A (page 4)
1. is
2. is
3. is
4. are

Exercise 6B (page 5)
1. 're
2. 're
3. 's
4. 're

Exercise 6C (page 5)
1. 'm; *many answers are possible.*
2. 'm; *many answers are possible.*

Exercise 6D (page 5)
1. my
2. His
3. Our
4. Our, Their

Exercise 7A (page 6)
1. yes
2. yes
3. no
4. yes
date, area code

Exercise 7B (page 6)
Many answers are possible but may include the following:
1. date
2. name
3. street address
4. city and state
5. zip code
6. telephone number (including area code)
7. languages spoken
8. job applying for

Exercise 7C (page 7)

Many answers are possible. Share your answers with another learner or your teacher. All required information should be provided. There should be no writing below the double dotted line.

Exercise 7D (page 7)

Many answers are possible. Share your answers with another learner or your teacher.
The interviewer

Exercise 8 (page 8)
1. an employee ID badge
2. the Human Resources Department

Exercise 9 (page 8)

Many answers are possible. Share your answers with another learner or your teacher.

Exercise 1A (page 9)
1. supply room
2. *Both answers are possible. Share your answers with another learner or your teacher.*
3. boxes

Exercise 1B (page 9)

Many answers are possible but may include the following:
supply room, break room, meeting room, rest room, parking lot, office, copy room, lunch room, classroom, secretary's office, computer room, library, Human Resources, Manager's/Supervisor's/Principal's Office, security

Exercise 2A (page 10)
1. break room
2. supply room
3. parking lot
4. rest room
5. meeting room
6. office

Exercise 2B (page 10)

Many answers are possible. Share your answers with another learner or your teacher.

Exercise 3A (page 11)

Many answers are possible. Share your answers with another learner or your teacher.

Exercise 3B (page 11)
1. left, first, left
2. down, third, right

Exercise 4 (page 11)

Many answers are possible. Share your answers with another learner or your teacher.

Exercise 5 (page 12)
1. the manager's office
2. the break room
3. the ladies' room
4. meeting room 2

Exercise 6A (page 12)
1. Yes, it is.
2. Yes, they are.
3. No, it isn't.
4. Yes, it is.

Exercise 6B (page 13)

Many answers are possible but may include the following:
1. Where's the men's room?
   It's next to the supply room. *or*
   It's on the left next to the exit.
2. Where's the manager's office?
   It's between the secretary's office and Human Resources. *or* It's the second door on the right.
3. Where's the break room?
   It's across the hall from the supply room.
4. Where's meeting room 1?
   It's across from the secretary's office. *or* It's the first room on the left.
5. Where's the computer room? It's next to human resources.

Exercise 6C (page 13)

Many answers are possible but may include the following:
Go down the hall. Turn left. The break room is on the right. It's across the hall from the supply room. *or* It's the first door on the right.

Exercise 7A (page 14)
1 pillow

Exercise 7B (page 15)
Many answers are possible. Share your answers with another learner or your teacher.

Exercise 7C (page 15)
Many answers are possible. Share your answers with another learner or your teacher.

Exercise 8 (page 16)
1. 320
2. 150
3. 250
4. 300
5. 170

Exercise 9 (page 16)
Many answers are possible. Share your answers with another learner or your teacher.

Exercise 1A (page 17)
1. c
2. a
3. d
4. b

Exercise 1B (page 17)
Many answers are possible. Share your answers with another learner or your teacher.

Exercise 2A (page 18)

Exercise 2B (page 18)
1. write a letter
2. send a fax
3. make coffee
4. add numbers

Exercise 3 (page 19)
1. START button
2. cover
3. glass

Exercise 4 (page 19)
Many answers are possible but may include the following:
1. Open the cover.
2. Put the paper on the glass.
3. Choose the number of copies.
4. Close the cover.
5. Press the START button.

Exercise 5 (page 20)
1. d
2. a
3. b
4. c

Exercise 6A (page 20)
1. 's telling
2. 're cleaning
3. 's not going
4. 're working
5. 'm not starting
6. 's repairing
7. 's talking

Exercise 6B (page 21)
1. What is she doing?
   She's fixing a car.
2. What is he doing?
   He's sending a fax.
3. What are they doing?
   They're sewing.
4. What are they doing?
   They're cooking.
Many answers are possible but may include the following:
1. Is she fixing a car? Yes, she is.
2. Is he sending a fax? Yes, he is.
3. Are they sewing? Yes, they are.
4. Are they cooking? Yes, they are.

Exercise 6C (page 22)
1. secretary's
2. manager's
3. job counselors'

Exercise 7A (page 22)
1. the cover
2. the ON/OFF switch
3. the bag
4. the ON/OFF switch

Exercise 7B (page 23)
Many answers are possible, but may include the following:
1. Plug in the coffee maker.
2. Pour water into the coffee maker.
3. Put coffee in the filter basket.
4. Press the ON button.

Exercise 8 (page 24)
1. You call 555-9090.
2. You check to see if the bag is full. If it is full, you change the bag.
3. You check to see if the switch is set to FLOORS.

Exercise 9 (page 24)
Many answers are possible. Share your answers with another learner or your teacher.

Exercise 1A (page 25)
1. yes
2. yes
3. yes
4. yes

Exercise 1B (page 25)
Many answers are possible. Share your answers with another learner or your teacher.

Exercise 2 (page 26)
1. 12:45
2. 6:20
3. 3:05
4. 4:15

Exercise 3A (page 26)
1. Tuesday
2. Sunday
3. Monday

4. Thursday
5. Friday
6. Saturday

Exercise 3B (page 27)
1. Monday
2. Thursday
3. Tuesday
4. *Many answers are possible.*
Many answers are possible. Share your answers with another learner or your teacher.

Exercise 4 (page 27)
A appointment
B time
A At
B late
A Thanks

Exercise 5 (page 28)

Copy Shop		
Schedule for week of __(date)__ to __(date)__		
Monday 9:00 – 5:00	**Tuesday** 10:30 – 6:30	**Wednesday** 8:30 – 5:30
Thursday 9:00 – 5:00	**Friday** 8:30 – 5:30	**Saturday** ———

Exercise 6A (page 28)
1. Can, can't
2. can, can, Can
3. can, can't, can
4. Can, can

Exercise 6B (page 29)
1. Monday
2. January
3. 1999

Exercise 6C (page 29)
1. Is it; Yes, it is.
2. Is it; No, it isn't.
3. Is it; No, it isn't.
4. Is it; No, it isn't.

Exercise 7A (page 30)
1. first
2. 4
3. no
4. Kevin
Maya. Maya isn't working on Friday. Maya has Friday off.

Exercise 7B (page 31)
(date)
Sunday: off
Monday: 10 to 6
Tuesday: 10 to 6
Wednesday: off
Thursday: 6 to 2
Friday: 6 to 2
Saturday: 3 to 11
Total: 40
1. *Many answers are possible but any time during the day on Monday through Friday is available.*
2. Wednesday, Sunday
3. Wednesday and Sunday

Exercise 7C (page 31)
All five items should be checked.
Many answers are possible but may include the following:
amount of work that needs to be done each day; if there are any holidays; if work should be scheduled for every day

Exercise 8 (page 32)
Many answers are possible but may include the following:
1. doctor's appointment
2. jury duty
3. illness
4. training class
5. teacher's conference
Many answers are possible. Share your answers with another learner or your teacher.

Exercise 9 (page 32)
Many answers are possible. Share your answers with another learner or your teacher.

U N I T ◆5◆

Exercise 1A (page 33)
1. yes
2. no
3. yes
4. no

Exercise 1B (page 33)
Circle b and d.

Exercise 2A (page 34)
1. help
2. may
3. Thank you
4. Welcome

Exercise 2B (page 34)
Many answers are possible but may include the following:
"Hello, how can I help you?
"Good morning, what can I do for you today?"

Exercise 3 (page 35)
1. c
2. a
3. b

Exercise 4 (page 35)
problem
sorry, refund
Sure, apology

Exercise 5 (page 36)
Norma Valdez
3 gallons of paint, $7.95, $23.85
10 boxes of nails, $5.75, $57.50
2 paintbrushes, $2.75, $5.50
$86.85

Exercise 6A (page 36)
some, a, an, some
a
an

Exercise 6B (page 37)
How much: paint, oil, juice, coffee, paper, money
How many: clocks, nails, cameras, photocopies, light bulbs, spark plugs

Exercise 6C (page 37)
How many
How many
How much
How many

Exercise 7A (page 38)
1. yes
2. yes
3. no
4. yes
Many answers are possible but may include the following:
apologize to the unhappy customer; offer help/refund/exchange
complain to the manager; ask for help

Answer Key

Exercise 7B (page 39)
1. c
2. a
3. b

Exercise 7C (page 39)
Many answers are possible but all information should be filled in, including descriptions of the following three problems.
There's a leak in the men's room.
Paper is coming out of the copier in the mail room.
The door to the break room is broken.

Exercise 8 (page 40)
1. no
2. no
3. yes
Circle 1 and 3.

Exercise 9 (page 40)
Many answers are possible. Share your answers with another learner or your teacher.

Exercise 1A (page 41)
1. Quality Car Rental
2. 7:00 a.m.
3. yes
4. yes
5. yes

Exercise 1B (page 41)
Many answers are possible. Share your answers with another learner or your teacher.

Exercise 2A (page 42)
1. bus driver
2. machinist
3. mechanic
4. truck driver

Exercise 2B (page 42)
1. no
2. yes
3. yes
4. no
Many answers are possible. Share your answers with another learner or your teacher.

Exercise 3 (page 43)
1. Excuse me
2. Certainly
3. Thank you
4. Ms.

Exercise 4 (page 43)
1. b
2. a
3. c
4. d

Exercise 5 (page 44)
1. a
2. b
3. b

Exercise 6A (page 44)
A this
B those
A those, these

Exercise 6B (page 45)
A does, start
B starts
A does, work
B works, do, leave
A leave

Exercise 6C (page 45)
1. A Does, walk
   B doesn't
2. A Do, come
   B do
3. A Does, open
   B does
4. A Do, work
   B *Answers will be either* Yes, I do. *or* No, I don't.

Exercise 7A (page 46)
1. cashier
2. usually
3. yes
4. yes
5. key
Yes
Many answers are possible but may include the following:
Sylvia is punctual. She arrives at work on time.

Sylvia is helpful. She helps other employees.

Sylvia is polite. She is pleasant to supervisors, coworkers, and customers.

Sylvia is flexible. She is willing to do different tasks.

Many answers are possible but may include the following:

Sylvia needs to remember her cash register key.

Exercise 7B (page 47)
Many answers are possible. Share your answers with another learner or your teacher.

Exercise 7C (page 47)
Many answers are possible. Share your answers with another learner or your teacher.

Exercise 8A (page 47)
1. b
2. a
3. b

Exercise 8B (page 48)
Many answers are possible but may include the following:

"Sure, what do you need to talk about?"

"OK, I can help you now."

Many answers are possible. Share your answers with another learner or your teacher.

Exercise 9 (page 48)
Many answers are possible. Share your answers with another learner or your teacher.

Exercise 1A (page 49)
1. bank
2. money
3. paycheck
4. deposit

Exercise 1B (page 49)
Many answers are possible. Share your answers with another learner or your teacher.

Exercise 2A (page 50)
1. f
2. d
3. a
4. e
5. b
6. c

Exercise 2B (page 50)
1. $30.55
2. $13.00
3. $ 9.03
4. $ 2.10

Exercise 3 (page 51)
1. yes
2. yes
3. no
4. yes

Many answers are possible but may include the following:

the days you work

the hours you work

your hourly pay rate

the total hours you work

your total pay

your signature

the date you sign the time card

Exercise 4A (page 51)
1. 7/21/99
2. Maria Bullock
3. 34.56
4. 381.34

Exercise 4B (page 52)

Exercise 5 (page 52)

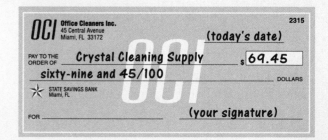

Exercise 6A (page 52)

1. How many bills are there? There are four bills.
2. How many time cards are there? There is one time card.
3. How many paychecks are there? There are six paychecks.

Exercise 6B (page 53)

A Are there
B there are
A Is there
B there isn't
A Is there
B there is

Exercise 6C (page 53)

1. Which check is for Restaurant Suppliers?
2. Which check is for $56.93?
3. Which check is from February 15?

Exercise 7A (page 54)

1. Tuesday, Thursday
2. Mark, the employee, and his supervisor
3. $5.55
4. 3:00
5. 12:00
6. 4
7. 35.5

Exercise 7B (page 54)

Many answers are possible. Share your answers with another learner or your teacher.

Exercise 7C (page 55)

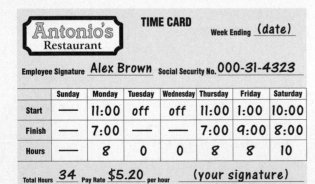

$176.80; no; learner should not sign the paycheck

Exercise 8 (page 56)

a. 1
b. 3
c. 5
d. 2

Many answers are possible. Share your answers with another learner or your teacher.

Exercise 9 (page 56)

Many answers are possible. Share your answers with another learner or your teacher.

U N I T 8

Exercise 1A (page 57)

1. b, d
2. a, b, c
3. b
4. d

Exercise 1B (page 57)

1. b, c
2. a

Exercise 2A (page 58)

1. eye
2. nose
3. throat
4. neck
5. stomach
6. arm
7. wrist
8. hand
9. finger
10. knee
11. ankle
12. toe

Exercise 2B (page 58)

eyes, feet, hands, head

Exercise 3 (page 59)

Many answers are possible but may include the following:

911: 911 operator. What's your name and phone number?
You: *Many answers are possible.*
911: What's the emergency?

You: A car is on fire in front of my house.
911: We'll send help right away. What's the address?
You: *Many answers are possible.*

Exercise 4 (page 59)
1. burn
2. sick
3. broken leg
4. stomachache

Exercise 5 (page 60)
1. a
2. c
3. a
4. b

Exercise 6A (page 60)
1. A do, feel
   B feel
2. A do, feel
   B feel
3. A does, feel
   B feels

Exercise 6B (page 61)
1. She has a headache.
2. He has a fever.
3. They have broken arms.
4. We have stomachaches.

Exercise 6C (page 61)
B feel, has, has
A feel, has

Exercise 7A (page 62)
Answers may vary. Share your answers with another learner or your teacher.
1. c
2. d
3. f
4. b

Exercise 7B (page 63)
1. work boots
2. gloves
3. wet
4. hard hat

Exercise 8 (page 64)
1. yes
2. no
3. yes
4. no
5. no

Exercise 9 (page 64)
Many answers are possible. Share your answers with another learner or your teacher.

U N I T 9

Exercise 1A (page 65)
1. yes
2. together
3. kitchen

Exercise 1B (page 65)
Many answers are possible. Share your answers with another learner or your teacher.

Exercise 2A (page 66)
1. c, e, i
2. a, f, g
3. b, d, h

Exercise 2B (page 66)
Many answers are possible. Share your answers with another learner or your teacher.

Exercise 3A (page 67)
a, c, d, h

Exercise 3B (page 67)
1. c
2. a
3. b

Exercise 3C (page 67)
Many answers are possible but may include the following:
1. Chen: I'm sorry. I won't be late again.
2. Marla: Thank you.
3. Fred: I'm sorry. I'm not usually so messy.

Exercise 4 (page 68)
1. a, c
2. a, b
3. b, c

Exercise 5A (page 68)
1. yes
2. no
3. yes
4. no
5. yes

Exercise 5B (page 68)

Many answers are possible. Share your answers with another learner or your teacher.

Exercise 6A (page 69)

Many answers are possible. Share your answers with another learner or your teacher.

Exercise 6B (page 69)

1. a. is working
   b. works
2. a. take
   b. am learning
3. a. trains
   b. is teaching
4. a. drive
   b. are taking

Exercise 6C (page 69)

Many answers are possible. Share your answers with another learner or your teacher.

Exercise 7A (page 70)

1. security guards
2. no
3. yes
4. 5
5. no
6. yes
7. 6
8. yes

Exercise 7B (page 71)

1. hat
2. black shirt
3. name tag
4. black pants
5. black shoes

Exercise 7C (page 71)

Many answers are possible. Share your answers with another learner or your teacher.

Exercise 8 (page 72)

Many answers are possible. Share your answers with another learner or your teacher.

Exercise 9 (page 72)

Many answers are possible. Share your answers with another learner or your teacher.

U N I T 10

Exercise 1 (page 73)

1. a
2. a
3. a
4. a

Many answers are possible but may include the following:
from friends or family; from notices on bulletin boards; from the Internet

Exercise 2A (page 74)

1. waiter
2. waitress
3. police officer
4. cook
5. cashier
6. delivery driver

Exercise 2B (page 74)

1. e
2. d
3. a
4. f
5. c
6. b

Exercise 3 (page 75)

B   studying, cook, doing
A   looking, bus

Many answers are possible. Share your answers with another learner or your teacher.

Exercise 4 (page 75)

1. medical technician
2. carpenter's helper
3. baker
4. gardener

Exercise 5 (page 76)

build a house
use tools
supervise workers

Exercise 6A (page 76)

B   can
A   can, can
B   Can
A   can't, can
B   can

Exercise 6B (page 77)

1. Was Pablo a truck driver?
   was
2. Were Hans and Marta painters?
   weren't
3. Was Sara a tailor?
   wasn't
4. Were you a mechanic?
   No, I wasn't. *or* Yes, I was.

Exercise 6C (page 77)

A   how long
B   was, to
A   How long
B   For, From

Exercise 7A (page 78)

Exercise 7B (page 78)

1. 555-2646
2. 555-3250
3. 555-1923
4. 555-1212

Exercise 7C (page 79)

Many answers are possible. Share your answers with another learner or your teacher.

Exercise 7D (page 79)

Many answers are possible. Share your answers with another learner or your teacher.

Exercise 8 (page 80)

Many answers are possible. Share your answers with another learner or your teacher.

Exercise 9 (page 80)

Many answers are possible. Share your answers with another learner or your teacher.

English ASAP™
Connecting English to the Workplace

———————— Literacy Level ————————

Student Book	0-8172-7950-4
Teacher's Edition	0-8172-7953-9
Audiocassettes	0-8172-7960-1

———————————— Level 1 ————————————

Student Book	0-8172-7951-2
Workbook	**0-8172-7956-3**
Teacher's Edition	0-8172-7954-7
Audiocassettes	0-8172-7961-X

———————————— Level 2 ————————————

Student Book	0-8172-7952-0
Workbook	0-8172-7957-1
Teacher's Edition	0-8172-7955-5
Audiocassettes	0-8172-7962-8

———————— Writing Dictionary ————————

Workforce Writing Dictionary	0-8172-7959-8

———————— Placement Tests ————————

Form A	0-8172-7971-7
Form B	0-8172-7972-5

STECK-VAUGHN®
COMPANY

A Division of Harcourt Brace & Company

ISBN 0-8172-7956-3

90000

9 780817 279561

Steck-Vaughn

English ASAP™

Connecting English to the Workplace